SCIENCE
FUN
COLOUR

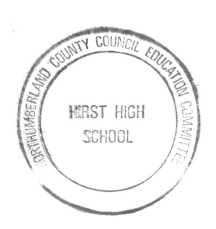

A DORLING KINDERSLEY BOOK

Project Editor Phil Wilkinson
Art Editors Peter Bailey
Photography Pete Gardner
Additional photography Dave King

First published in Great Britain in 1991 by
Dorling Kindersley Limited,
9 Henrietta Street, London WC2E 8PS

Paperback edition
2 4 6 8 10 9 7 5 3 1

Copyright ©1991, 1998 *illustrations*
Dorling Kindersley Limited, London
Copyright © 1991, 1998 *text* Neil Ardley

Visit us on the World Wide Web at
http://www.dk.com

A CIP catalogue record for this book is available
from the British Library

ISBN 0-7513-58185

Reproduced in Hong Kong by Bright Arts
Printed in Belgium by Proost

SCIENCE
FUN
COLOUR

Written by
Neil Ardley

DORLING KINDERSLEY
LONDON • NEW YORK • MOSCOW • SYDNEY

What is colour?

Imagine a world without colour. It would be like living in an old movie. Colour brings everything to life. All light contains colour - the white light from the sun contains all the colours of the rainbow. But when light shines on an object, only some colours bounce off it. Our eyes detect the colours in light coming from objects, and we see things in colour. So grass looks green because green light comes from it. Colour is important for plants and animals. Flowers, for example, have brilliant petals that attract insects bringing pollen so they can form seeds.

CD rainbow
The surface of a compact disc changes white light to rainbow colours.

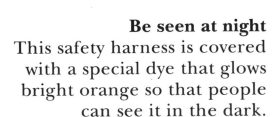

Red for danger
Colours often have meanings. Red usually means danger, perhaps because it is the colour of blood. Red and green mean stop and go in traffic signals.

Be seen at night
This safety harness is covered with a special dye that glows bright orange so that people can see it in the dark.

Finding a mate

Many birds display bright colours to attract or warn off other birds. The brilliant colours in a peacock's tail attract the female.

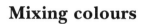

Mixing colours

When this wheel spins, the coloured dots merge to make other colours. Television, photography, and printing bring us pictures in colour by mixing just three basic colours!

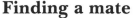 This sign means **take care**. You should ask an adult to help you with this step of the experiment.

Be a safe scientist
Follow all the directions carefully and always take care, especially with glass, scissors, matches, candles, and electricity. Never put anything in your mouth or eyes. Pour away water and coloured liquids when you finish, and switch off torches and electric lights when you have finished with them. Never touch electric light bulbs - they get very hot.

Make a rainbow

Why do rainbows appear in the sky? In this experiment you can turn white light from a torch into all the colours of the rainbow.

You will need:

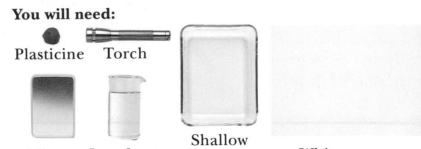

Plasticine Torch

Mirror Jar of water Shallow dish White paper

Use the plasticine to attach the mirror to one end of the dish.

1 Half fill the dish with water.

2 Put the mirror in the dish so that it slopes back.

3 Hold the torch near the dish. Shine its light on the part of the mirror under the water.

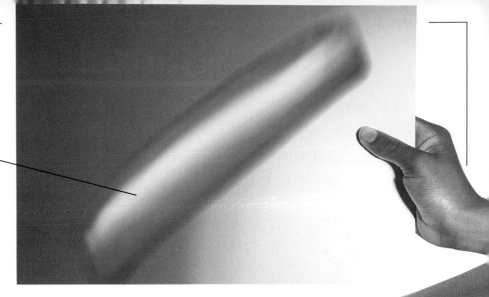

White light splits into a range of colours, from blue to red.

4 Hold the piece of white paper above the torch. A rainbow appears on the paper.

Moving or tilting the torch may help you see the rainbow.

Curve of colours
When the sun is shining and it is raining, the raindrops split up the sun's white light into different colours. This forms the rainbow. The same thing happens with the torch and the water in the dish.

Sunset

The sky often goes orange or red when the sun sets. Find out why the sky changes colour in this way by making an orange and red sunset from white milk and water.

You will need:

Water

Milk

Torch

Spoon

White light from the torch

1 Shine the torch through the water on to a white wall. It gives a white light.

2 Add a little milk to the water.

3 Stir the milky water with the spoon.

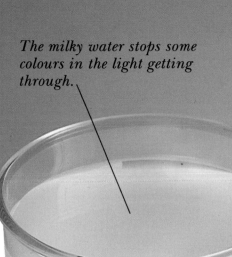

The milky water stops some colours in the light getting through.

Only orange and red light rays pass through the milky water to reach the wall.

4 Now shine the torch through the white milky water. The wall lights up with an orange-red colour!

Red sky at night

White light from the sun passes through the air. At sunset, only orange and red rays get through the air. Tiny particles in the air stop all the other colours. The sun looks orange-red and it lights up the clouds with an orange-red colour.

Colours from nowhere

Make bright colours appear in clear plastic. You will see how some sunglasses can do more than reduce the sun's glare. They cut out some of the colours in white light, leaving others to reach the eyes.

You will need:

Polarizing sunglasses

Plastic cassette box

Lamp

2 Look at the box through the sunglasses.

1 Place the opened cassette box on a table and line up the lamp to light the box. Switch on.

3 Bright colours appear in the plastic!

Breaking point
Scientists make models in clear plastic, and use polarized colours to show where they might break.

Colour box

Why does a red object look red? Because red light bounces off its surface. The object soaks up all the other colours in the white light falling on it.

You will need:

Sticky tape

Red handkerchief

White paper

Torch

Box

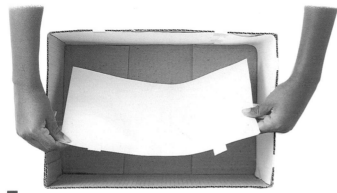

1 Stick the white paper to the inner sides of the box.

2 Spread out the handkerchief to cover the bottom of the box.

3 Shine the torch close to the handkerchief. The sides of the box turn deep red. You can try handkerchiefs in other colours.

Red light bouncing off the surface of the handkerchief lights up the sides of the box.

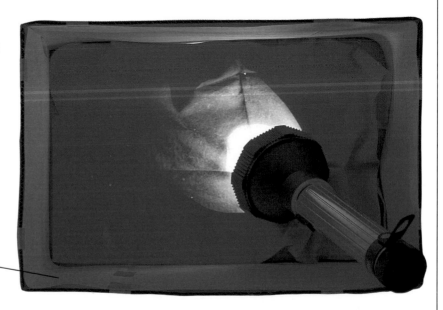

Coloured lights and shadows

Light up your hand in different colours and see coloured shadows appear. You can do this by using pieces of coloured plastic to change ordinary white lamps into ones that give off coloured light. You will see how light can change colour as it passes through coloured things.

You will need:

Red and blue plastic folders

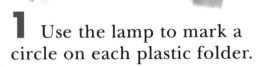 Scissors

 Sticky tape

Two lamps

Make sure that the lamps are not plugged in.

1 Use the lamp to mark a circle on each plastic folder.

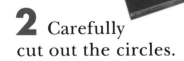

2 Carefully cut out the circles.

The bulb must not touch the plastic.

3 ⚠ Tape the circles to the lamps and ask an adult to plug in and switch one lamp on.

4 Shine the lamp on a white surface. Its red light makes your hand go red with a dark shadow.

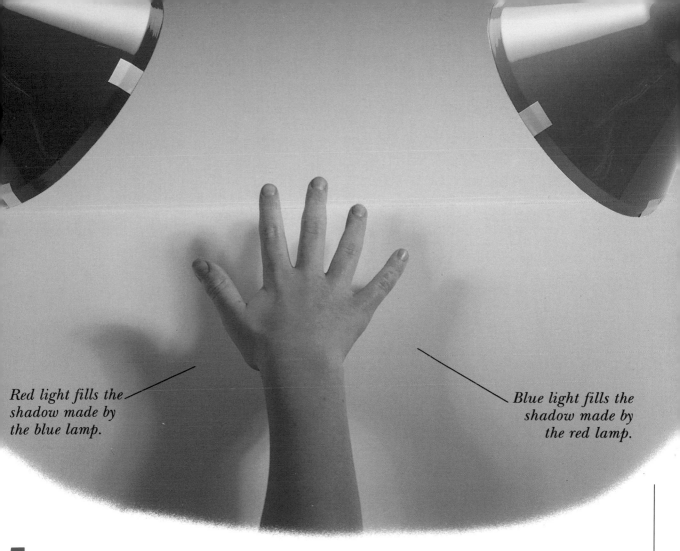

Red light fills the shadow made by the blue lamp.

Blue light fills the shadow made by the red lamp.

5 Ask an adult to plug in the other lamp and switch on. Shine both lamps on your hand. It goes red and blue with two shadows, one blue, one red.

On stage
Stage lamps produce bright beams of coloured light to give fantastic colour effects. In each lamp, white light from a bulb strikes a plastic sheet of a certain colour. The plastic stops all the other colours in the white light, and lets only that colour pass through.

Mixing colours

Pictures in books can show all the colours of the rainbow. Yet they contain only three colours! Use the plastic from some folders to show how these colours mix to give other colours.

You will need:

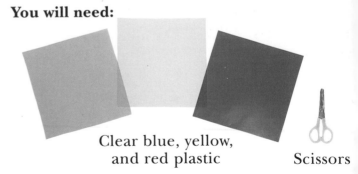

Clear blue, yellow, and red plastic

Scissors

1 Cut out some strips of coloured plastic.

2 Working on a white surface, lay a yellow strip over a blue strip. See how green appears where the strips overlap.

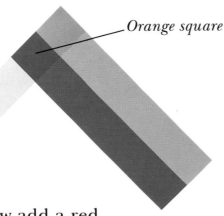

Orange square

3 Now add a red strip. See how yellow and red make orange.

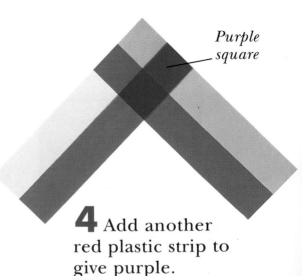

Purple square

4 Add another red plastic strip to give purple.

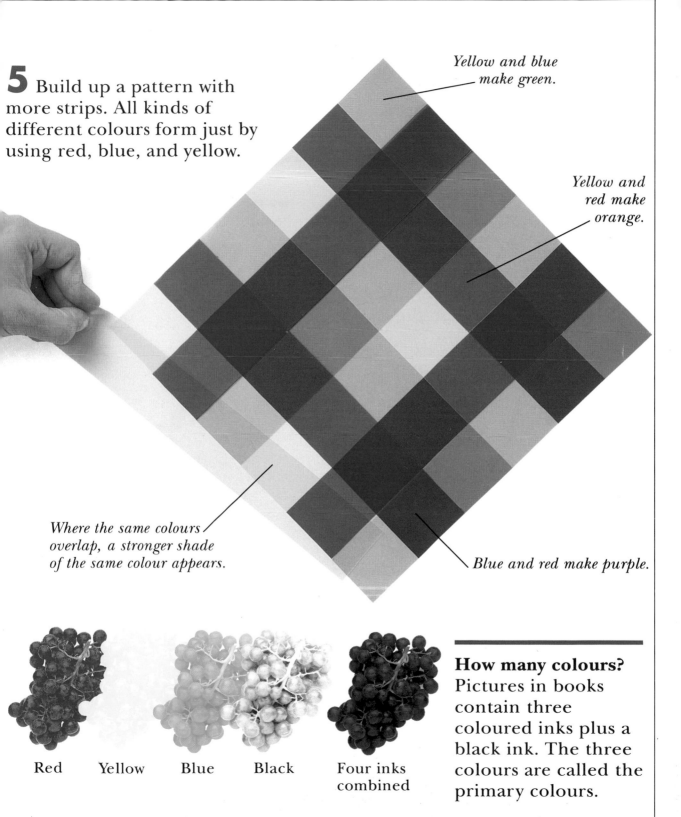

5 Build up a pattern with more strips. All kinds of different colours form just by using red, blue, and yellow.

Yellow and blue make green.

Yellow and red make orange.

Where the same colours overlap, a stronger shade of the same colour appears.

Blue and red make purple.

Red   Yellow   Blue   Black   Four inks combined

How many colours? Pictures in books contain three coloured inks plus a black ink. The three colours are called the primary colours.

Circle of colour

Fool your eyes into seeing many different colours when in fact only red, green, and blue light comes to your eyes. This is also what happens when you watch colour television.

You will need:

Scissors

Compasses

Green, red, and blue pens

Pencil

White card

1 Using the compasses, draw a circle on the card.

2 Carefully cut out the circle of card.

3 Using the three coloured pens, mark dots of red, green, and blue on the circle.

4 Push the pencil through the centre of the circle.

The dots of red, green, and blue appear to spread out and form rings.

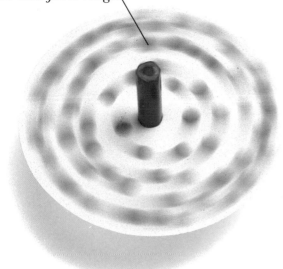

5 Spin the circle like a top. Rings of different colours appear!

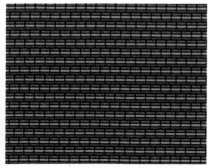

Patchwork picture
Examine a colour television set with a magnifying glass. The picture is made of tiny patches that light up in red, green, and blue. The patches merge togther when you look at the screen from a distance. Light of the three colours mixes to give all the colours in the picture.

Hidden colours

Some colours are not what they seem. You can show that they are made of lots of different colours mixed together. It's easy to find the hidden colours in the inks in felt-tip pens.

You will need:

Felt-tip pens

Blotting paper

Bowl of water

Pegs or clips

Thread or string   Scissors

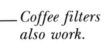

Coffee filters also work.

1 Cut the blotting paper into strips.

2 Draw a circle near the bottom of each strip.

3 Tie the string to some supports to keep it in place above the bowl. Attach the strips of paper to the string. Arrange them so that the water touches the bottom edges but does not touch the ink.

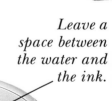

Leave a space between the water and the ink.

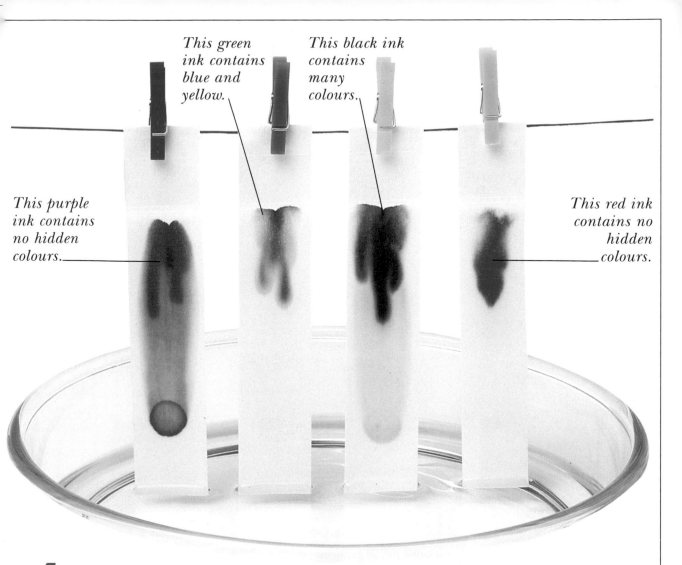

This green ink contains blue and yellow.

This black ink contains many colours.

This purple ink contains no hidden colours.

This red ink contains no hidden colours.

4 The water moves up the paper. Colours move different distances with the water, and each ink may separate into several colours.

Making paints

Paints come in many different shades of colour, but in fact they contain hidden colours. Paints are made by mixing pigments of several basic colours together in different amounts. Artists mix paints together in a similar way when they paint a picture.

Colour test

Things can suddenly change colour as if by magic. You can make some colour changes, and use them as a test.

You will need:

Knife   Soap   Lemon

Large jars   Small jars   Funnel   Red cabbage   Filter paper

Use the funnel and filter paper to strain the juice.

3 Add lemon juice to one jar.

1 ⚠ Pour warm water on to some chopped red cabbage. Let it sit for a few minutes.

2 Strain the cabbage juice. Pour some of it into the small jars.

4 Add some soap to another jar of cabbage juice and stir.

Lemon is an acid. It turns the juice red.

This jar contains only cabbage juice.

Soap is an alkali. It turns the juice green.

5 The colour of the cabbage juice changes from its usual purple to other colours.

Compare the colours of the two jars with a jar containing nothing but cabbage juice.

Try adding other things. Acids turn the juice red and alkalis turn it green or blue.

Other things to test
Vinegar
Bicarbonate of soda
Baking powder
Washing-up liquid
Ammonia
Grapefruit juice
Apple juice
Fizzy drinks

Living colour test
Soil may contain acids or alkalis. Hydrangeas have blue flowers in acid soil, but pink flowers in alkaline soil. Adding acid or alkali to the soil can make these flowers change colour.

23

Invisible ink

Send a secret message or code number to a friend using invisible ink. Using a special colour change, your friend will be able to see the message or code appear on the paper.

You will need:

Brush

Dish

Lemon

Tincture of iodine

White paper   Dropper   Bottle

1 Squeeze the lemon juice into the dish.

Store the iodine in a safe place.

2 ⚠ Put some water into the bottle. Ask an adult to add a little iodine using the dropper.

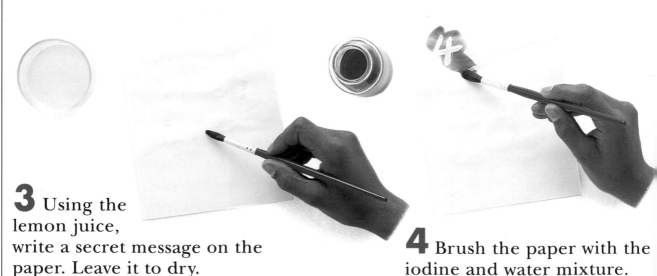

3 Using the lemon juice, write a secret message on the paper. Leave it to dry.

4 Brush the paper with the iodine and water mixture.

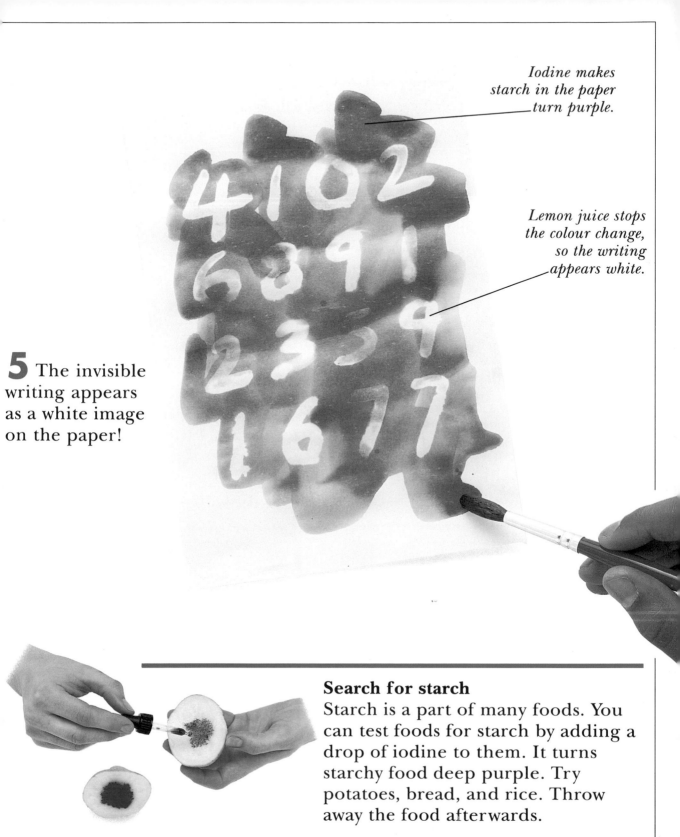

*Iodine makes
starch in the paper
turn purple.*

*Lemon juice stops
the colour change,
so the writing
appears white.*

5 The invisible
writing appears
as a white image
on the paper!

Search for starch

Starch is a part of many foods. You
can test foods for starch by adding a
drop of iodine to them. It turns
starchy food deep purple. Try
potatoes, bread, and rice. Throw
away the food afterwards.

Printing patterns

You can print brilliant coloured patterns on paper by using oil, water, and paint. You will get a different pattern each time you try. You will also see how printing transfers coloured inks to paper.

You will need:

Palette

Linseed oil
(or white spirit)

Paper

Bowl of water

Brush

Poster paints

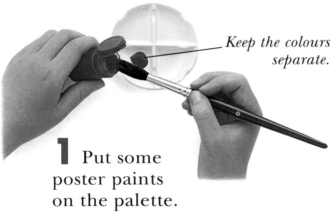

Keep the colours separate.

1 Put some poster paints on the palette.

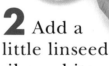

2 Add a little linseed oil or white spirit to each colour and stir well.

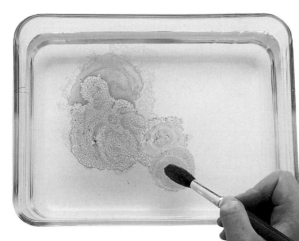

3 Take some colour on your brush and drop it gently on to the water.

4 Do the same with other colours. Push the colours around to give a pattern.

5 Lay a sheet of paper down carefully on top of the colour.

6 Carefully peel the paper away from the surface of the water.

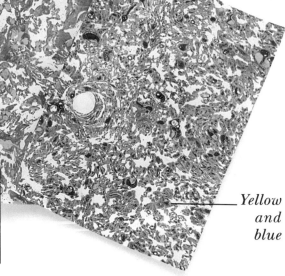

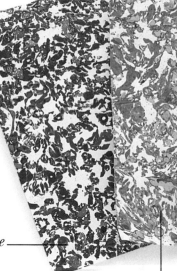

7 Leave the paper to dry on a flat surface. Print some more patterns using different colour combinations.

Red and blue

Red and yellow

Yellow and blue

Printing press
Some printing machines use a similar method to this experiment. An image is drawn on the printing plate in a greasy material. The plate is put in water, and the printing ink only attaches itself to the greasy areas, which repel the water.

Making colours

Use some vegetables to make your own dyes. These home-made dyes give pale shades, unlike the strong colours of modern, artificial dyes.

You will need:

Clean white cotton handkerchiefs

Saucepan

Rubber gloves

Large bowl

Beetroot slices

Strainer

Onion skins

1 ⚠ Put the onion skins in the saucepan and cover them with water. Ask an adult to boil them for 15 minutes. Then leave the pan to cool.

2 Pour the liquid through the strainer into the bowl.

Clear yellow dye

3 Put on the rubber gloves and dip the handkerchief into the liquid.

4 Squeeze out the handkerchief. Lay it on a clean sheet of paper to dry.

Handkerchief dyed with beetroot

Handkerchief dyed with onion skins

5 Repeat steps 1 to 4 with the beetroot. The colours may fade or wash out.

Powder paints

Long ago, people made paints by crushing coloured rocks and mixing the powder with oil. This red comes from a rock called cinnabar.

Picture credits
(Picture credits abbreviation key: B=below, C=centre, L=left, R=right, T=top)

Pete Gardner: 6BR, 7CL; The Image Bank: 6CL, 9BL, 13BL; Colin Keates: 29CL; ICI Paints: 21BL; London Features International Ltd./David Koppel: 15BL; Nimbus Records: 6TL; Pershke Price Service Organisation Ltd.: 27BL; Science Photo Library/Peter Aprahamian/ Sharples Stress Engineers Ltd: 10BL; Vaughan Fleming: 19BL; Jerry Young: 7TR

Picture research Cynthia Hole

Title page photography Dave King

Dorling Kindersley would like to thank Claire Gillard for editorial assistance and Mark Regardsoe for design assistance; Mrs Bradbury, the staff and children of Allfarthing Junior School, Wandsworth, especially Joe Armstrong, Mark Baker, Melanie Best, Damien Francis and Alice Watling.